*Trusting God's Love to Overcome Life's Challenges*

# REKINDLING MY ROSE PETALS

MICHELE CLARICE HARMON

REKINDLING MY ROSE PETALS

Printed in the United States of America.
ISBN: 979-8-9925317-4-9



PurposePals Publishing books may be ordered through booksellers or by contacting PurposePals.
hello@purposepalsllc.com
purposepalsllc.com

# Dedication

*To those whose journey has felt like a garden filled with thorns, may this story remind you that every rose blooms in its own time. May you find strength, purpose, and peace in God's unending love.*

*This book is dedicated to the women who feel broken, yet rise. To the dreamers, believers, and seekers of faith who continue to bloom despite life's storms. You are never alone on this journey.*

*For my family, friends, and loved ones who have shown me the beauty in every season of life. And to God, the constant gardener of my heart, who nurtures and loves each of His roses, even through the roughest winters.*

# My Prayer

Dear Lord,

Thank You for everything You have done for me so far in my life. I am so grateful for Your constant presence, love, and guidance. Please continue to watch over me and lead me in every direction You have planned for my life. Protect my heart, soul, and mind from negativity so it will not harm me or interfere with my spiritual growth.

I thank You for every high and low I've experienced—each one has shaped me into the woman I am today. I now see myself as a blessed, beautiful woman, gifted with many talents and a heart full of love.

Thank You for the precious blessing of my children, Akyma, Akari, and Amonte, as well as my brother and his beautiful daughters, Riley and Ramona. I am beyond grateful for the gift of family. Lord, I also thank You for my two dear friends, Courtney and Raynardia, whom You've placed in my life. Their love, support, and friendship mean more to me than words can express. Please continue to watch over all of them—mentally, physically, and spiritually. Keep them safe and cover their lives with Your peace and protection.

Lord, I am Yours. Thank You for Your endless love and support. I know there are moments when I feel lost and unsure of my next steps, but I trust You completely. Continue to uplift me and show me the path You have set for me. Use me, Lord, as a vessel of hope and encouragement, that I may be a blessing to others in every way possible.

I pray for wisdom, good health, peace, and happiness over my life, my family, my friends, and their loved ones. Protect us, Lord, from the evil and hatred present in this world. Surround us with Your light, love, and grace. In Jesus name, Amen.

In Jesus' name, Amen. 

# Foreword

Rekindling My Rose Petals is a must read that will touch the lives of so many individuals from adults to adolescence. This is the kind of read everyone needs on their bookshelf as a direct go to book to always reference. Michele Harmon is a phenomenal woman with a heart bigger than the world and us in it. This book is a true testimony of how God works through us and the abundance of love fulfilled with accepting Him as our Savior.

Michele has always been a light in my life and over the last 20 years of friendship, I'm so grateful she trusted me alongside her journey and walk with God. She has given me so much enlightenment just by being an honest person and supportive in my life and to many others she holds close to her.

Every chapter down to every page of Rekindling My Rose Petals has me finding myself more encouraged, uplifted, and eager to continue to read more. I especially enjoyed the Pruning for Growth segment where she talked about having to leave things and people behind to move forward. "It's like pruning a rosebush. To bloom fully, the dead or diseased buds must be cut away so the healthy branches can thrive"-Michele Harmon

This was a hard pill to swallow throughout different trials in my life and to be able to have that reassurance that certain decisions we make may not be easy, but necessary, felt good to be able to relate to having another person with the same views conveyed in a spiritual fashion that I instantly connected with.

I can relate to everything she referred to in her book, and I know many of you will too. I am so proud of you for sharing this gift with everyone. To give a piece of yourself so near and dear to the world is yet another selfless act that makes you the Child of God that you are.

Rekindling My Rose Petals symbolizes what His unwavering love looks like, and the author reminds us that we are enough for God and that alone fills my heart with pure joy. Michele is not only my best friend, but she is also my lifeline. As I go through life's challenges, I'm forever grateful to have a true friend in the battlefield with me whom I can always lean on to share the Lord's faith and love with. Rekindling My Rose Petals is a revival to the mind and soul and will have you feeling recharged and reminded on how God's love is endless. She reminds us in such a beautiful way to understand our worth is enough to Christ and that it's never too late to regrow or start over just like planting a rose from a single bud. I pray God continue to use you as a vessel with this book and to give readers hope and restored faith, allowing your light to everyone to shine bright through any darkness with your love.

-Coco 

# Acknowledgments

This journey would not have been possible without the unwavering support, love, and encouragement of so many people. To my family, who has been my constant source of strength and inspiration, thank you for standing by me through every challenge and triumph. Your love has been the soil that has allowed me to grow.

To my friends, Coco, Raynardia, and Kimi who have cheered me on and believed in my vision even on the days I doubted myself—thank you for your endless encouragement and understanding. Each of you has taught me something precious about resilience and grace.

A heartfelt thank you to my publisher, Kimi Johnson, who saw the heart of this story and helped me bring it to life with clarity and passion. Your guidance has been invaluable, and I am so grateful for your patience and insight.

To my faith community and mentors, thank you for your wisdom and for nurturing my spiritual growth. This book is as much a testament to your influence as it is to my personal journey.

Above all, I give my deepest thanks to God, whose presence and love have been my foundation and compass through every step. This book exists because of His grace, and it is dedicated to sharing the light and hope I have found in Him.

# Reflections

# Planting the Seed

Embracing Identity and Beginning Spiritual Renewal

# The Introduction

There's a beauty in blooming—one that doesn't come without struggle, pain, and growth. Rekindling My Rose Petals was born from a season of transformation, a deeply personal journey where I rediscovered my faith, my strength, and my purpose. For years, I carried the weight of loss, heartbreak, and self-doubt. I wrestled with my identity, questioned my worth, and wondered if I could ever truly heal. But through it all, God never left my side.

This book is not just my story—it's a testimony of God's grace, patience, and unwavering love. Like a rose, I've learned that true growth requires pruning. There were moments when I felt stripped bare, broken, and unsure if I could keep going. But God was there, gently removing what no longer served me, cutting away fears, toxic relationships, and habits that kept me from blooming fully.

And in the stillness, He reminded me: You are not forgotten. You are being made new. This collection of reflections is a celebration of both the thorns and the petals—of the struggles that shape us and the beauty that comes from healing. Each chapter shares moments of raw honesty, personal growth, and spiritual awakening. I've included scripture, personal experiences, and heartfelt encouragement with the hope that my journey will inspire you to embrace your own.

You'll find themes of faith, forgiveness, self-discovery, and God's perfect timing woven throughout these pages. I've learned that healing requires honesty—being willing to look in the mirror and confront both our brokenness and our beauty. It demands trust, a surrendering of

control, and a belief that God is working, even when life feels messy. I don't have all the answers. I'm still learning, still growing, still blooming.

But one truth remains unshaken: God's love is constant. His grace is sufficient. And no matter how far you feel, no matter how broken your petals may seem—He is in the process of making you whole again. As you read these words, my prayer is that you'll feel seen, encouraged, and reminded that you are never alone. This journey isn't about perfection. It's about transformation—one step, one prayer, one bloom at a time.

Thank you for allowing me to share my heart with you. May these words water the soil of your spirit and remind you that you, too, are beautifully and wonderfully made.

With faith and love,
Michele Harmon

# All Roses are Unique

Each rose is a masterpiece—one of a kind, created by the divine hand of God. This uniqueness, this singularity, is how God made us. Just as no two roses are identical, no two souls share the same journey or purpose. We are each a precious bloom in God's garden, growing at our own pace, in our own way.

To me, uniqueness means being made in a way that cannot be duplicated. Every person is designed with a distinct identity, a set of qualities, and a purpose that no one else can fulfill. This truth becomes especially evident in my faith journey, where I've come to understand that no two lives are identical. Even when others face similar struggles or challenges, the outcomes vary because God's plan for each of us is beautifully different. My growth, healing, and blessings are shaped not by coincidence but by how deeply I trust and stay connected with Him.

***Jeremiah 29:11 reminds us of this truth: "For I know the plans I have for you, declares the Lord, plans to prosper you and not to harm you, plans to give you a future filled with hope."***

Gardener is always near, ensuring we have what we need to grow—His love, His Word, His Spirit.

I've seen this in my own life. When I became a mother, and later when I had to step into the role of a mother figure for my brother after the passing of our parents, I realized God had entrusted me with a profound purpose—to nurture, protect, and guide, even when I felt lost and heartbroken. I didn't feel equipped for the task, yet God's strength filled the gaps where I felt weak. He placed in me the gifts of compassion, leadership, and resilience, showing me that purpose often reveals itself most clearly during trials.

Reflecting on God's design in my life is something I try to do intentionally. Prayer has been my anchor—it's in those quiet moments, when I allow the Holy Spirit to move in my heart, that I feel most in tune with His plans. Surrounding myself with prayer warriors and keeping a spirit of gratitude reminds me that God is always working, even when I can't see the full picture. The many blessings I've experienced, both big and small, are evidence of His hand at work.

I've also drawn strength from the "roses" God has placed in my life. My grandmothers, both deeply spiritual women, modeled unwavering faith. Their stories, biblical teachings, and the ways they lived out God's love taught me powerful lessons about prayer, giving, and serving my community. Their faith left an imprint on me—reminding me that we don't just bloom for ourselves but to offer beauty, encouragement, and hope to those around us.

Still, I'll admit there have been moments when I've fallen into the trap of comparison. I've wondered why my growth looked different from others or why certain struggles seemed heavier on my path. But I've learned that comparison often steals joy—it can lead to discouragement, isolation, and self-doubt. Yet, when viewed with the right perspective, it can also inspire self-reflection and motivate personal growth. The key is staying rooted in truth: God's plan for my life is unique, and my worth is not measured against someone else's bloom.

So, I choose to embrace the beauty of my own unfolding. I am not meant to look like anyone else's rose, and neither are you. Our lives, our faith journeys, and our growth all reflect the creativity of a God who delights in diversity. Together, we make a breathtaking garden—each bloom precious, each story sacred.

And so, I encourage you: Let God nurture you where you are. Trust His timing. Celebrate the ways you're growing, even when the petals feel slow to unfurl. Because you, too, are a masterpiece—one of a kind, perfectly designed by the Master Gardener.

Self Love:
Everyday look in the mirror and say Hello Beautiful! Gods loves me for Who I Am with all my flaws and beautiful talents.

# Rose Petal Reflections

# Rose Petal Reflections

# Rose Petal Reflections

# Rose Petal Reflections

# Rose Petal Reflections

# Rose Petal Reflections

# Rose Petal Reflections

# Looking in the Mirror

The mirror doesn't lie. It reflects truths we often try to bury—the truths we don't want to see but desperately need to face.

For a long time, I avoided my own reflection. When I did dare to look, I saw a woman consumed by guilt, fear, and regret. I felt trapped in my mistakes, haunted by choices I couldn't undo. I was angry, ashamed, and lost in my faith. But even as I wrestled with those heavy emotions, I realized something: avoiding the truth didn't change it. If I wanted healing—if I wanted to grow—I had to be ready and willing to do the hard work of uncovering the real me. So, I looked closer.

At first, all I saw was brokenness—a Black woman overwhelmed by her pain, drowning in sadness and self-doubt. I felt the weight of every mistake, every misstep, every tear-soaked night where I questioned my worth. My reflection reminded me of all my flaws and failures, and for a while, that was all I could see. But then, something shifted.

Somewhere beneath the pain, I caught a glimpse of someone else—a woman with purpose, a woman filled with potential, a woman God had chosen for something greater.

Facing myself fully meant confronting both realities: the hurt and the hope, the brokenness and the beauty. It was agonizing, but it was necessary. I had to learn to forgive myself. To forgive others. And to hand the weight of my pain over to God.

Self-forgiveness became central to my healing. I had to reevaluate my life, face the truth about my past decisions, and admit that some of the pain I carried came from choices I made. That was hard to accept. I felt guilt, shame, disappointment—even disgust. But avoiding my reflection wouldn't bring healing. I had to face it, own it, and trust that God's grace was bigger than my mistakes.

When I looked deeper, beyond the hurt, I saw a woman with dreams. A woman with a caring heart. A woman God hadn't abandoned, even when I had felt unworthy of His love.

Still, there were days when the weight of self-doubt clung heavily to my spirit. On those days, my mind felt clouded, my heart overwhelmed.

***Philippians 4:6-7 became a lifeline during that season:***
***"Do not be anxious about anything, but in every situation, by prayer and petition, with thanksgiving, present your requests to God. And the peace of God, which transcends all understanding, will guard your hearts and minds in Christ Jesus."***

I struggled to focus, lost sleep, and even lost my appetite. My spirit felt too heavy to be around others, even those I loved. But God met me in that space.

I found comfort in prayer and meditation, seeking God's presence when my heart felt too broken for words. His presence became my refuge, my safe place. There, in the quiet, I discovered that healing isn't about perfection—it's about surrender.

Working through guilt and sadness hasn't been easy. I've had to learn to sit with my feelings, not run from them. To acknowledge the pain but not let it define me. I still have moments when I question myself—when I feel the sting of old wounds reopening. But instead of turning away from the mirror, I'm learning to face it head-on.

Because now, when I look closely, I don't just see my brokenness. I see a woman being rebuilt by grace. I see strength where there once was shame. I see growth where there once was guilt. I see the undeniable evidence of a God who doesn't just heal—He transforms. This journey isn't about being flawless. It's about being faithful. So, when the mirror feels unbearable, I encourage you to look deeper. Don't turn away. God isn't finished with you yet. You are loved. You are chosen. And you are still becoming.

Get it Out!!
Get a journal and
start writing to God!
Write your feelings,
prayers and thoughts
to God. Don't be
afraid!

# Rose Petal Reflections

# Rose Petal Reflections

# Rose Petal Reflections

# Rose Petal Reflections

# Rose Petal Reflections

# Rose Petal Reflections

# Rose Petal Reflections

# Taking Root

Establishing a Foundation of Faith and Trust

# Why Me?

There was a time I asked myself that question repeatedly—Why me? Why did life feel so overwhelming, so unfair? It's easy to feel lost when the weight of your struggles feels like too much to bear. I've learned, though, through pain and growth, that this journey was never mine to walk alone. It's always been me and God, side by side, even when I couldn't feel His presence.

The battles I face—whether mental, emotional, or spiritual—aren't meant to break me. They are tests of my faith. And while God already knows the outcome, He wants me to grow, to rise, to see who I become when I face those challenges head-on.

There was a time when I didn't understand that. I felt abandoned, overwhelmed, and defeated. I kept asking, Why me?—especially during moments of heartbreak and loss. Losing my parents, navigating failed friendships, going through divorce, and struggling with my identity as a Black woman in this world left me feeling unsteady, questioning my worth and my purpose.

But one of the most painful times was losing my mother. I was just 21 years old, with three young children under the age of five, and suddenly, I had to step into the role of both sister and mother for my 11-year-old brother. I was heartbroken, lost, and scared. I kept asking God why He would take someone so beautiful, so full of life, from us. I wanted her back so badly that I isolated myself from my family. I withdrew, sinking into depression, blinded by grief.

I see now that while my pain was real, my perspective was limited. I

was holding on to my mother, not realizing she was already at peace, in the arms of God—where her faith had promised she would be. I couldn't see it then, but God was with me too. What felt like abandonment was actually preparation. He was strengthening me for the life ahead, shaping me with compassion, resilience, and grace.

In time, the answer to Why me? shifted quietly, almost imperceptibly, into Why not me?

Why not be the one to rise stronger? Why not be the one God trusts to carry a testimony of faith and endurance? I have a purpose, and even when I don't fully understand my path, I am confident in this: I am loved. I am chosen. I am enough in God's eyes.

Today, when I wrestle with moments of feeling alone, I'm reminded that I'm never truly by myself. God is present—faithful and steady—even in the silence. I've learned to seek His presence intentionally. Prayer has become my lifeline, a place where I can pour out my heart without fear of judgment. I've also learned the power of simply being still, listening for His quiet whispers in the moments when life feels the loudest.

Practically, I've found peace in simple ways—long walks in nature, sitting by the water, journaling, and surrounding myself with positive people who uplift my spirit. Therapy has also been a healing space for me, a reminder that seeking help doesn't diminish my faith but strengthens it.

Still, there are moments when the silence feels deafening—when

I'm desperate for answers and God seems distant. In those moments, my spirit feels fragile, and my anxiety creeps in, making my heart feel unsteady. But I've learned something important: silence doesn't mean absence. Even when I don't hear Him, God is working.

The enemy would love to use those moments of quiet to fill my mind with fear, self-doubt, and negativity. But I've discovered that staying rooted in prayer, gratitude, and God's promises makes all the difference. His Word reminds me that His timing is perfect, His love unwavering. I may not always understand the why, but I can trust that He is faithful, and His plans for me are good.

So, if you've ever found yourself asking Why me?, know this: You are not forgotten. You are not alone. God is working, even when you can't see it. And through every struggle, He is shaping you into the beautiful masterpiece you were created to be.

***Silence doesn't mean absence.***
***Even when I don't hear Him, God is working.***

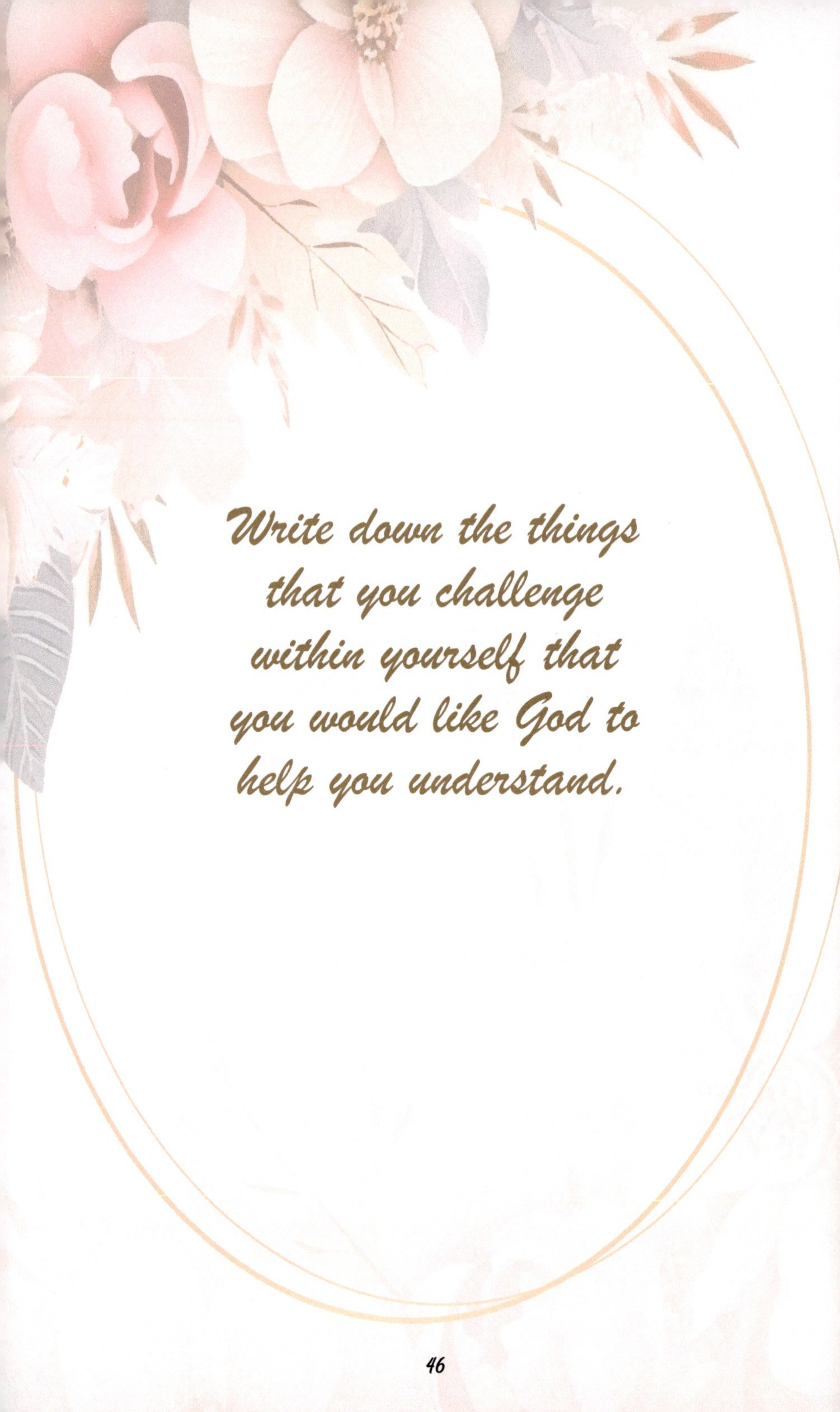

*Write down the things that you challenge within yourself that you would like God to help you understand.*

Rose Petal Reflections

Rose Petal Reflections

Rose Petal Reflections

Rose Petal Reflections

# Rose Petal Reflections

# Rose Petal Reflections

Rose Petal Reflections

# Facing the Thorns

No journey with God is without its thorns. Life has a way of pressing us, stretching us, and testing us in ways we never imagined possible. I've felt those thorns—sharp, unrelenting, piercing the tenderest parts of my heart. Parenthood, the loss of my parents, the heartbreak of divorce after thirteen years of marriage, and losing my child's father to suicide all left me feeling as though I was walking through fire. There were moments when my faith felt fragile, stretched thin by grief and unanswered questions. I often found myself backed into a corner, questioning God, questioning my strength, questioning… everything.

But even in those moments of deep pain, when the weight felt unbearable, I've learned a truth that changed everything: God never left my side. Though I couldn't always see a way out, He was there. Constant. Steady. Present. His love wasn't loud or forceful—it was a quiet strength, a whisper reminding me, You are not alone. Trusting Him completely wasn't easy. My pain made me crave answers, not silence. But over time, I've come to understand that silence doesn't mean absence. Sometimes His presence is found in the stillness, in the spaces where words fail, and all that's left is the steady assurance that He is with me.

Joshua 1:9 became my anchor in those seasons of brokenness: "Be strong and courageous. Do not be afraid; do not be discouraged, for the Lord your God will be with you wherever you go." Even in the midst of life's thorns, God has never left.

Finding strength during trials isn't a one-time decision—it's a daily choice. I've learned that staying connected to God requires intention, especially when life feels overwhelming. Some days, it means whispering simple prayers through tears. Other days, it means pouring my heart out in journaling or simply sitting quietly, letting His peace fill the empty spaces in my heart. I've stayed grounded by talking to God daily, not with rehearsed prayers, but with raw, vulnerable honesty. I've turned to moments of meditation and reflection, where silence creates room for me to listen instead of always speaking. His Word has also been a lifeline—reading scripture and letting His truth anchor me when my emotions feel louder than my faith. Staying connected to positive influences, being part of a faith community, and surrounding myself with people who encourage my spiritual walk have also helped me stay strong, even when life feels uncertain.

In my hardest moments, I've clung tightly to the words of the Serenity Prayer.

***God, grant me the serenity***
***To accept the things I cannot change,***
***Courage to change the things I can,***
***And wisdom to know the difference.***

Those words reminded me that not everything is mine to carry—some burdens belong at the feet of Jesus. Learning to release control, to surrender the weight of my worries, brought me peace, even when I didn't have all the answers.

While my faith has been my foundation, God has also blessed me with an incredible support system—my children and my brother. Their presence alone brings light into my darkest moments. When life feels unbearable, when the heaviness tries to consume me, seeing their faces reminds me why I keep pressing forward. Their love gives me strength, even when my spirit feels fragile.

Beyond my family, God has placed amazing friends in my life—my childhood friends and my life coach, Coco, Raynardia, Lateshia, and Kimi. They've been unwavering in their support, showing up for me in every season of heartache and healing. Whether it was my divorce, the loss of my parents, or personal milestones like going back to school after more than fifteen years, their encouragement has been a constant

reminder that I am not alone. They have covered me in prayer, spoken life over me, and held space for me when words felt impossible. Each one has a special place in my heart, and words fall short when I try to express the depth of my gratitude for them.

Lately, I've found myself leaning more into solitude—not out of isolation, but out of a deep longing to hear God's voice clearly. I've discovered a sacred peace in being alone with Him, pouring out every hurt, every question, and allowing His presence to meet me there. It's in those quiet spaces—where the world feels miles away—that I've come to understand the difference between being alone and being with God.

The thorns of life may pierce deeply, but they cannot destroy me. They've shown me that even in brokenness, God's grace is still at work—refining, restoring, and preparing me for something greater.

So if you find yourself in a season of thorns, wondering if the pain will ever end, I encourage you—hold on. Trust that even when it feels like too much, when the answers seem far away, God is right there. Steadying you. Guiding you. Reminding you—You are never alone.

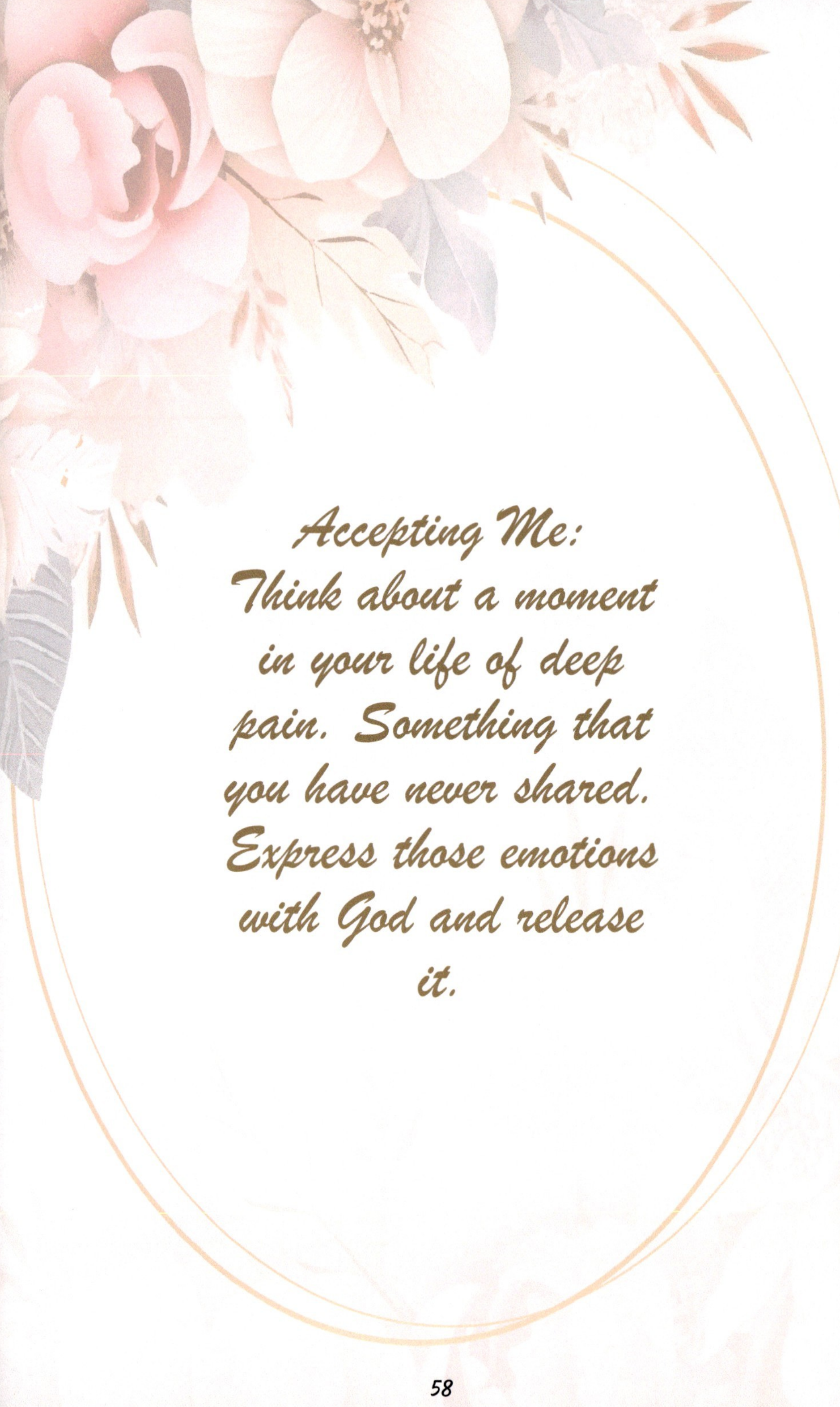

Accepting Me:
Think about a moment in your life of deep pain. Something that you have never shared. Express those emotions with God and release it.

Rose Petal Reflections

Rose Petal Reflections

# Rose Petal Reflections

Rose Petal Reflections

# Rose Petal Reflections

Rose Petal Reflections

# Rose Petal Reflections

# Be Quiet and Pray

Sometimes, silence speaks louder than words. I've learned to embrace solitude not as a sign of loneliness but as a sacred space where I can reconnect with God in the most honest and vulnerable way.

In those quiet moments—whether kneeling in prayer, sitting still in my car, or walking along a peaceful trail—I've found healing. Silence has allowed me to be raw, stripped of pretense, and completely transparent with God. I've prayed. I've cried. I've laid every fear, every insecurity, and every desire at His feet. And in return, I've discovered a quiet strength rising within me, a strength I knew wasn't my own.

Opening my heart that fully wasn't easy. Vulnerability is uncomfortable, even in prayer. But I've come to realize God doesn't need polished words or rehearsed prayers. He wants sincerity. He wants the truth—the real me. Prayer has become more than just a practice for me. It's my lifeline, a sacred exchange where I can lay down the weight of life and let God carry what was never mine to hold.

Philippians 4:6-7 reminds me of this truth: "Do not be anxious about anything, but in every situation, by prayer and petition, with thanksgiving, present your requests to God."

God desires our honesty. He wants us to come to Him completely, holding nothing back.

There are certain places where I feel closest to Him—where the noise of life quiets just enough for me to hear His voice. The local parks and nature trails have become sanctuaries for my soul. Sitting in my car

with the windows down, listening to the birds sing, or feeling the breeze on my face as I walk along a peaceful path brings me clarity. In those moments of stillness, I reflect, ask questions, and seek His guidance.

And He speaks. Not audibly, but spiritually—through a calm reassurance, a gentle nudge reminding me, I am here. Keep trusting.

Being alone with God isn't about silence for its own sake. It's about making space for His presence.

My relationship with prayer is still growing. It's far from perfect, but it's deepening. I've learned that God isn't looking for perfection—He's looking for persistence. I pray throughout my day, whether my spirit feels strong or fragile. Even on the days when my faith feels shaky, I've learned to praise Him anyway—because He's good, even when life isn't.

There have been moments when I couldn't find the words to speak aloud, so I wrote them down instead. Journaling my prayers has become a place where I can release everything I'm carrying, documenting my struggles and victories, and seeing how God has moved in my life over time. When I look back, those pages remind me that God was faithful then—and He will be faithful now. But prayer is more than words. It's surrender.

The hardest part of silent prayer isn't the quiet—it's the letting go. To be still before God means releasing my grip, laying down my plans, and trusting His will completely. It means surrendering my timeline and accepting His perfect timing, even when it feels painfully delayed.

I've wrestled with unanswered prayers. I've pleaded for God to move faster—to fix situations, to change outcomes, to bring clarity when everything felt unclear. But I've learned something powerful: unanswered prayers aren't the same as unheard prayers. Sometimes silence doesn't mean abandonment. It means God is working in ways we can't yet see.

It's not easy. But faith was never meant to be easy. Faith is trusting God's plan when you don't understand it.

Silence has become my greatest teacher. It's taught me that honesty with God is essential—He cannot heal what we refuse to reveal. I've learned that stillness has power, that the world's noise often drowns

***Proverbs 3:5-6 speaks directly to this truth: "Trust in the Lord with all your heart and lean not on your own understanding; in all your ways submit to Him, and He will make your paths straight."***

out His gentle whispers, and that waiting on God is an act of faith, not failure. So now, I lean into the quiet. I trust that even when the answers seem slow, God is working.

If you're in a season of silence, I want to encourage you—don't mistake it for God's absence. Let the quiet be a space where you press in deeper, where you give Him your rawest prayers, your deepest hurts, and your greatest hopes. Trust that He's listening, even when the stillness feels heavy. Because it's in that quiet space where transformation begins.

Mindful Prayer:
Spend 5-10 minutes daily in prayer or meditation with God! Be very detailed in your prayer!
Burn candles or essential oils to help with healing and positive energy.

Rose Petal Reflections

# Rose Petal Reflections

Rose Petal Reflections

Rose Petal Reflections

# Rose Petal Reflections

# Pruning for Growth

Letting Go and Trusting God's Refining Process

# Removing the Buds

God doesn't want us to remain stagnant. He calls us to grow, to become more like Him, and sometimes that growth requires the painful process of letting go—of people, habits, and mindsets that no longer serve our spiritual health.

It's like pruning a rosebush. To bloom fully, the dead or diseased buds must be cut away so the healthy branches can thrive. And while the pruning feels painful, it's necessary.

I've experienced this pruning firsthand. God has removed relationships, patterns, and behaviors from my life that were hindering my growth. Negative thoughts I clung to, grudges I held too tightly, and even unhealthy habits that felt like comforts—all had to be surrendered. Letting go of pain, resentment, and the desire to control outcomes wasn't easy. For a long time, I resisted, believing that holding on was somehow safer. But God was calling me higher, and I couldn't reach the next level of healing while dragging around the weight of things that no longer fit where He was taking me.

Letting go has never been easy for me. When God began to remove certain relationships, beliefs, and habits from my life, my initial reaction wasn't grace—it was grief. I felt hurt, disappointed, and even betrayed. Friendships shifted. People I once trusted faded from my life. There were moments when I questioned God, asking why He would allow these losses. It felt like rejection, even when, deep down, I knew He was protecting me from things I couldn't yet see.

But through the pain, I've learned a truth I now hold close: God

never removes without purpose.

There were people and patterns in my life that, while once familiar, were no longer healthy for my spiritual growth. I had to trust that when God closed a door, it wasn't out of cruelty but to create space for greater peace, healing, and purpose.

The process of removing these spiritual "buds" has taught me some hard but necessary lessons. Pain isn't pointless. Releasing toxic patterns often brings grief, discomfort, and confusion—but it also brings clarity. Not everyone can go where God is leading you, no matter how deeply you care. Some relationships and habits are meant for a season, not a lifetime. I've also learned that forgiveness is the key to freedom. Holding onto past hurts only kept me bound, but when I chose to release those wounds, true healing began.

One of the hardest lessons I've learned is that unhealthy behaviors can block blessings. Whether it's unhealthy attachments, self-doubt, or negative self-talk, those things can keep you stuck in cycles God never intended for you. I've had to remind myself often: You can't fully bloom while holding onto dead buds.

At first, I didn't always recognize when God was pruning. Sometimes, it wasn't obvious until life felt completely out of balance—when peace seemed out of reach, and confusion lingered. It was only then, in the discomfort, that I realized God was calling me to release what was no longer meant for my life.

Letting go was hard. I wrestled with the discomfort, questioning

why certain people were being removed, why familiar places suddenly felt foreign, and why I felt so emotionally stretched. But through prayer and patience, I've come to trust the process.

Peace, I've learned, often comes after surrender. When you finally stop clinging to what feels familiar and release it fully into God's hands, there's a shift. The pain gives way to healing. The anger softens. The confusion begins to clear. What once felt like loss reveals itself as preparation.

God's pruning was never meant to harm me—it was meant to help me thrive.

Yes, there have been relationships I've had to walk away from, influences I've had to release—jealous friendships, toxic family dynamics, unhealthy behaviors that once felt comfortable. Cutting those ties wasn't easy, especially when the connections felt deep. But God showed me that not everything is meant to stay forever. Some things, some people, are seasonal. Clinging to them only delayed my growth. But here's the beauty: when God removes, He also restores.

He may take away unhealthy relationships, but He brings new connections—friends who speak life and encouragement into my spirit. He may call you to leave a toxic environment, but He will lead you into spaces where you can flourish.

So, if you're in a season where God is pruning—where life feels uncomfortable, and the weight of letting go feels heavy—know this: You are not being punished. You are being prepared.

The discomfort you feel now is making space for something greater. Trust His timing. Trust His process. Trust that He is shaping you into a masterpiece—one cut, one bloom, one breakthrough at a time.

Because when you finally let go, you'll discover that peace, joy, and growth were always part of His plan for you.

Letting Go:
Before bed, reflect on your life and consciously let go of any negative thoughts or habits that may impact your spiritual development.

# Rose Petal Reflections

# Rose Petal Reflections

# Rose Petal Reflections

# Rose Petal Reflections

# Rose Petal Reflections

# Rose Petal Reflections

# Rose Petal Reflections

# Time for Fresh Soil

Building a new life often means starting from scratch. It can feel uncomfortable, even messy—like planting a seed in fresh soil. The ground has to be broken, the dirt turned, and the roots pressed deep so the seed can grow strong enough to endure life's storms. Spiritual growth works the same way. God calls us to invest in our faith, to get our hands dirty in the work of becoming who He created us to be. Growth rarely happens in comfort. It requires effort—prayer, patience, and a willingness to trust God's process, even when it feels uncertain.

As we grow, God continues to prune. Some things will fall away. Some relationships will shift. Parts of life that once felt familiar may no longer fit where God is leading. It can be painful, but it's necessary. With each shift, we move closer to becoming the person He has called us to be.

When I began to rekindle my faith, I knew I couldn't stay the same. My heart needed fresh habits, new patterns—intentional ways to draw closer to God. I started small but stayed consistent, carving out time each day to meditate and sit in stillness, allowing space to reflect, pray, and listen. I began journaling, writing out my prayers, struggles, and moments of gratitude, watching how my faith was growing with each page I filled. I took weekly walks on nature trails, letting God's creation clear my mind as I processed the lessons He was teaching me. Daily prayer became a lifeline, not just in moments of crisis but as a way to keep my heart open to His voice. I sought guidance from my life coach, read scripture more intentionally, and began speaking life over

myself—affirming God's truth about my worth and His plan for me.

These small shifts didn't just alter my daily routine—they transformed my spirit. They reminded me that growth isn't about perfection but progress, staying connected to God in both the quiet moments and the challenging ones.

But spiritual growth isn't always peaceful. There were moments when it felt like everything around me was shifting too fast. Friendships changed. Some relationships grew distant. Certain habits and patterns I once clung to no longer fit the life I was building with God. That kind of change stings. It feels like loss, even when you know it's necessary.

I had to learn that not everyone is meant to stay with you during your spiritual transformation. Some people won't understand the path God has placed you on. Some will question the changes in you, while others will fade quietly from your life. And while that shift can feel lonely, I've come to realize it's often part of God's plan. He creates space—not to leave you empty, but to make room for peace, healing, and the right people to enter your life.

Yes, the loneliness is real. But so is God's presence. When you lean into Him fully, you begin to understand that you're never truly alone. His love is constant, even when the crowd thins.

Rebuilding my life—both spiritually and personally—didn't happen overnight. It took time. And the truth is, I'm still a work in progress. Spiritually, I've deepened my relationship with God through intentional prayer, talking to Him openly, without holding back. I've

connected with spiritually-minded friends, mentors, and faith leaders who encourage my walk with God. Immersing myself in scripture has become essential, not just reading the words but seeking to understand His promises for my life. I've also learned the power of speaking life—declaring God's blessings over my family, my career, my health, and my purpose.

Externally, I've worked to reflect my inner growth in my daily life. I've become more involved in my community, serving others with kindness and compassion. I've made a conscious effort to live with integrity, aligning my words and actions with God's principles, even when it feels challenging. And I've had to release toxic spaces and relationships—letting go of anything that didn't bring peace or reflect God's presence in my life.

The process hasn't been perfect. I've stumbled. I've doubted. But through it all, God has remained faithful, gently reminding me that true growth takes time.

I've learned to stay rooted by remaining in God's Word, keeping my spirit grounded in truth. I've had to practice letting go of what no longer serves me, trusting that when I release what holds me back, I make space for new blessings. Gratitude has become essential—focusing not on what I lack but on how far God has already brought me. Daily prayer and moments of quiet reflection have kept me steady, reminding me that God's voice is often clearest in the stillness.

I've made a commitment to reflect His love wherever I go, showing

kindness and compassion, not just in words but in how I treat others. Growth can be uncomfortable. Change can feel painful. But God's pruning isn't punishment—it's preparation. He's preparing you for greater peace. He's preparing you for deeper faith. He's preparing you for the life He designed for you from the very beginning.

So if you feel like you're in a season where everything is being uprooted—trust the process. Trust the breaking. Trust the discomfort.

***Faith, like a garden, needs ongoing care. You don't stop watering a plant just because it begins to bloom. The same is true for spiritual growth. Let God do His work in the soil of your soul. Because what He's planting in you is going to bloom beautifully.***

My personal Time:
Find a new habit to start reconnecting with God such writing or having a life coach.

# Rose Petal Reflections

# Rose Petal Reflections

# Rose Petal Reflections

# Rose Petal Reflections

# Rose Petal Reflections

# Rose Petal Reflections

# Rose Petal Reflections

# Just Beautiful

Reconnecting with God has been the most beautiful transformation of my life. Through both struggles and moments of joy, I've begun to see myself differently—through His eyes. Not as someone defined by mistakes or haunted by past fears, but as someone beautiful, whole, and uniquely created. His love has revealed to me that I am not a reflection of my flaws. I am fully loved, completely accepted, and unconditionally cherished—even in my imperfections.

This journey hasn't been about striving for perfection. It's been about perspective. Learning to see myself the way God does has reshaped the way I view not only myself but others. I've come to understand that true beauty isn't measured by how the world defines it. It's not found in flawless appearances, designer clothes, or the image we present to others. Real beauty is deeper—rooted in the heart, in the quiet strength of a soul transformed by God's love.

Scripture captures this truth so well in 1 Peter 3:3-4:

***"Do not let your adornment be merely outward—arranging the hair, wearing gold, or putting on fine apparel—rather let it be the hidden person of the heart, with the incorruptible beauty of a gentle and quiet spirit, which is very precious in the sight of God."***

When I finally allowed God's love to fill my heart, it softened me in ways I never expected. His grace taught me to accept myself fully—flaws, mistakes, and all. Because if the Creator of the universe can look at me, in all my struggles, and still call me loved, worthy, and enough—how could I do anything less for myself?

Unconditional love, to me, is pure and limitless. It doesn't come with conditions, expectations, or requirements. It just is. It's the love God extends to us daily—the kind of love that whispers:

- You don't have to be perfect to be chosen.
- You don't have to have it all together to be worthy.
- You are enough, just as you are.

This love has changed not only how I see myself but how I see others. It has helped me become more compassionate, more patient, more forgiving. I've realized that everyone carries their own burdens, faces their own silent battles. And if God can love me so completely despite my imperfections, then I'm called to extend that same grace to those around me.

This newfound self-love has shown up in my life in ways I never imagined. I feel overjoyed and filled with gratitude—not because life is

perfect, but because I've finally learned to rest in God's love. I've let go of the need for constant approval and the exhausting burden of perfection. Instead, I've chosen to speak life over myself, reminding my heart that I am beautifully made in God's image. I've learned to extend grace to others, offering kindness and compassion instead of judgment. Gratitude has become my daily practice, shifting my focus from what I lack to the countless blessings already surrounding me. And I've learned to honor my worth by setting healthy boundaries and seeking relationships that reflect God's peace and love.

If you've ever doubted your beauty or your worth, I want you to know this:

- You are not defined by your past.
- You are not limited by your mistakes.
- You are not broken beyond repair.
- You are a masterpiece, handcrafted by God.

***And when you begin to see yourself the way He does—beautiful, whole, and deeply loved—there's a peace that no circumstance can shake.***

Remember you are Loved!!
Surround yourself around your love one and true friend.
Show yourself gratitude in your everyday life.

# Rose Petal Reflections

# Rose Petal Reflections

# Rose Petal Reflections

# Rose Petal Reflections

# Rose Petal Reflections

# Rose Petal Reflections

# Rose Petal Reflections

# Bloominng in Faith

Living with Gratitude, Growth,
and Spiritual Wholeness

# Maintenance is Needed

Maintenance is needed for spiritual growth. It's not a one-time event but a continuous process that requires daily care—prayer, gratitude, and a heart willing to serve others. Just like a rose needs regular tending to bloom, our souls need intentional nourishment to stay rooted in God's will.

I've learned that staying connected to God after intense moments of growth requires persistence, especially when life feels overwhelming. During those hard days, when my heart is vulnerable and my spirit feels fragile, I draw even closer to God. He is the constant presence that never fails me, never lets me down. Even when my days feel chaotic, I've learned the importance of praising Him anyway—showing gratitude not just for the good moments but for His unwavering love through the storms.

Since I've rekindled my focus on God, I've noticed a transformation in how I approach life. My spiritual growth continues, not because life has become easier but because my perspective has shifted. I see situations more clearly, recognizing that everything—whether good or challenging—is part of the process. God works in His own timing, and just because things don't move the way I expect doesn't mean His plan isn't unfolding perfectly.

I often reflect on the miracle when Jesus fed the multitudes with just a few fish and loaves of bread. He didn't complain about what seemed insufficient; He gave thanks. And He didn't hesitate when He

sacrificed His life for us. That truth has taught me to stop questioning my challenges and instead express gratitude, trusting that God is shaping something greater through every experience.

Looking back, my most profound spiritual growth came during a season of deep loneliness. After 13 years of marriage, I found myself separated, my kids had left for college, and the silence of my home felt unbearable. I was so used to being a mother and wife—managing school events, cooking dinner, helping with homework, and playing the role of caretaker—that when everything shifted, I didn't know who I was anymore. The sudden stillness left me feeling lost, hurt, and completely unprepared for the emotional toll it would take.

At first, I coped by staying busy—working long hours, avoiding home, distancing myself from friends and family. But no matter how much I distracted myself, the heaviness lingered. Sleepless nights, overwhelming sadness, and feelings of isolation consumed me. I didn't realize it in the moment, but those tears, those silent prayers in the middle of the night, were the very beginning of my spiritual transformation.

I reached a breaking point where I knew I couldn't keep living like that. I needed help, and not just temporary comfort—I needed God.

Prayer became my lifeline. I started journaling, pouring out my heart on paper, speaking honestly with God about my pain, my fears, and the healing I longed for. Gratitude followed. I began thanking Him—not just for the blessings I could see but for the strength I knew He was

building in me through my struggles.

That gratitude and prayer didn't just change my circumstances—they changed me. It's amazing how different life feels when you begin to thank God in all situations, not just the good ones. Gratitude has shifted my entire mindset:

- It deepens my spiritual connection with God.
- It opens the door for greater blessings.
- It helps me focus on positive thoughts.
- It reduces stress and anxiety.
- It brings peace to my mind and spirit.
- It strengthens my relationships with friends and family.

Even when life isn't perfect—and it rarely is—I've learned to stay rooted in daily prayer and gratitude. They are my spiritual maintenance, the tools that keep me aligned with God's purpose for my life.

But I'll be honest—there are moments when I feel spiritually drained. Burnout happens. When it does, I've learned how important it is to pause and reset. Sometimes, that means taking a short trip or isolating myself for a few days to recharge my mind and spirit. I avoid distractions and focus on spiritual practices that restore my soul—prayer, meditation, journaling, and even burning sage as a symbolic act

of cleansing and clarity.

What keeps me spiritually motivated, even during those difficult seasons, is surrounding myself with the right people—positive influences and prayer warriors who speak life into me. My children are also a constant source of motivation. Just hearing their voices or spending time together reminds me why it's so important to stay spiritually grounded.

I've found peace in simple joys too—writing in my journal, standing by the ocean, listening to the waves as they remind me of God's vastness and steady presence. Maintaining spiritual growth isn't about being perfect. It's about being consistent. Staying connected. Staying grateful. Staying open to the work God is doing, even when the process feels slow.

***Just like a rose, when we tend our faith daily, the beauty of our growth will eventually bloom for all to see.***

Nourishing your spirit:
Incorporate an act of
kindness to others.

Rose Petal Reflections

Rose Petal Reflections

# Rose Petal Reflections

Rose Petal Reflections

Rose Petal Reflections

# Rose Petal Reflections

# Rose Petal Reflections

# Thank you, God I'm Still Blooming

Being able to see another day is a blessing I no longer take for granted. Each morning brings new opportunities—to grow, to learn from my mistakes, and to keep becoming the person God created me to be.

Life hasn't been without its challenges, but every obstacle has taught me the importance of staying on the path God designed for me. True growth requires accountability—being honest with yourself, acknowledging where you've fallen short, and allowing God to shape you in the process. For so long, I struggled to see clearly, weighed down by pain and self-doubt. But now, I thank God for opening my eyes, helping me view my life with clarity, positivity, and a heart full of gratitude. When you truly connect with God, peace and joy follow. He knows exactly what your spirit needs to thrive on this journey.

I've come to realize that spiritual growth is a lifelong journey, not a single destination. It requires dedication—to the process, to healing, and to rebuilding your relationship with God. But you have to be ready. You have to be willing to face yourself, fully and honestly, without fear. There were parts of my story I once felt ashamed of—mistakes I wanted to forget. But I've learned that facing those moments with courage is part of the process of spiritual development.

Life, as complicated as it feels sometimes, is also incredibly precious. God's design is perfect, even when we can't see the full picture. I've learned that some of the challenges I've faced weren't punishments—

they were lessons. Sometimes we try to make decisions in our own strength instead of seeking His wisdom. And yet, through it all, God has been faithful. He allows us to face struggles not to break us but to see how we respond—to teach us trust, dependence, and unwavering faith.

He is always in control. And your life, no matter how difficult it seems, is designed with purpose. Looking back, I see how far God has brought me.

I'm no longer the person I once was—the one who felt defeated, overwhelmed, and bitter. Today, I see a believer who has grown stronger, clearer, and more confident in both faith and purpose. I've become a prayer warrior, no longer trying to handle life's challenges alone but trusting God fully.

My perspective has changed too. I approach decisions with greater peace, no longer driven by fear but by faith. My heart is more humble, more compassionate, filled with love and kindness toward others. Emotionally, I'm in a healthier place than I've been in years. There was a time when I felt so burdened that I relied on anxiety and depression medication just to cope. But through God's grace, I no longer need those things to find peace. Writing my prayers in my journal has become my therapy—my way of releasing burdens and finding clarity. There's something powerful about putting my thoughts on paper, watching my progress, and seeing how God has moved in my life. If I could offer you one piece of advice, it would be this: Don't give up.

God is your greatest supporter—your #1 cheerleader. Even when life feels overwhelming, even when the answers feel far away, He is working. Keep your head up. Speak life over yourself—over your mind, your health, your relationships, and your purpose. Pray. Then pray some more.

I express my gratitude to God not just in words but in how I live. I thank Him for His mercy, for the strength He's given me, and for never turning away from me, even when I struggled to see my own worth. Every day, I strive to reflect His love—through kindness, compassion, and the way I encourage those around me.

I feel overjoyed knowing that God is still working in me—that He continues to give me the grace to bloom, one day at a time.

Life isn't easy, but every blessing and lesson is worth it when you're walking by faith.

Waking up each morning is a privilege. And with every sunrise, I'm learning more, drawing closer, and experiencing the beauty of a relationship with God. His love is unconditional. His presence is unmatched. And because of Him—I'm still blooming.

***"Dear Lord, thank You for the growth and strength You've given me. Continue to watch over my life and guide me on this spiritual journey. Help me become a better version of myself—one rooted in Your love and truth. Thank You for the lessons, the struggles, and the victories that have shaped me. Amen."***

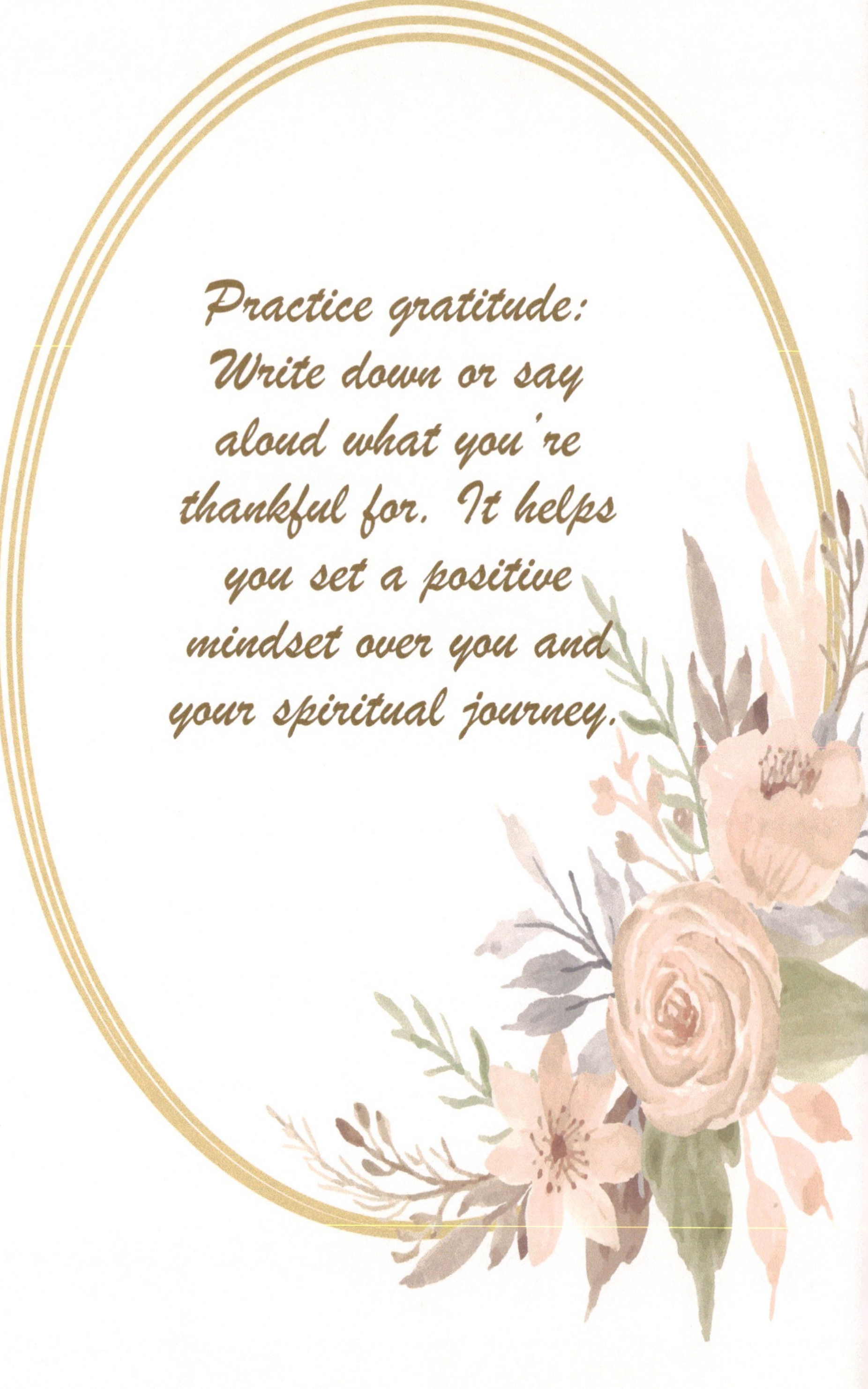

Practice gratitude: Write down or say aloud what you're thankful for. It helps you set a positive mindset over you and your spiritual journey.

# Rose Petal Reflections

# Rose Petal Reflections

# Rose Petal Reflections

Rose Petal Reflections

# Rose Petal Reflections

# Rose Petal Reflections

Rose Petal Reflections

# About the Author

Michele Harmon is an inspiring author, mother, and trusted friend whose mission is to empower others to reconnect with their true selves and embrace God's love. With a heart devoted to helping others on their faith journeys, Michele has spent over two decades navigating the complexities of life, from personal challenges to spiritual growth. Through her own experiences of loss, transformation, and self-discovery, she has learned the power of faith and the importance of trusting in God's plan.

Michele's writing draws from her personal story of healing and strength, inviting readers to find peace in the midst of struggle and to understand the beauty of their own unique path. When she's not writing, Michele enjoys spending time with her family, traveling, and encouraging others to find ways to enjoy life. "Rekindling My Rose Petals" is her first book, and she hopes it serves as a source of inspiration and guidance for anyone seeking to deepen their spiritual journey and rediscover their true beauty in God's eyes.

Contact Michele by email at: jazzyjmj@gmail.com

Made in the USA
Columbia, SC
30 March 2025

73410c69-2df5-42f5-96ed-0d5b24828839R01